JUGGLING
& FEATS OF
DEXTERITY

JUGGLING

& FEATS OF DEXTERITY

Gay to say how do you do.
And introduce myself to you.

A BULFINCH PRESS BOOK
Little, Brown and Company
Boston · Toronto · London

First United States Edition

ISBN 0-8212-2048-9

Library of Congress Catalog Card Number 93-71052

*Bulfinch Press is an imprint and trademark of
Little, Brown and Company (Inc.)*

Editorial Director: MADAME JOANNA LORENZ
Creative Director: SIR PETER BRIDGEWATER
Text: PAUL BARNETT and RON TINER ESQUIRES
Original Illustrations: COLONEL IVAN HISSEY
Design Magicians: SIMON BALLEY, ANNIE MOSS,
FRANCES MARR AND TERRY JEAVONS
Assisted by: JANE LANAWAY

*The Publishers would like to thank all those who kindly gave
permission to use visual materials in this book.*

PRINTED IN HONG KONG

Contents

INTRODUCTION: AN ADMONITORY ANECDOTE 6

JUGGLING WITH SCARVES, NAPKINS or KERCHIEFS 9

THE CASCADE 12

THE CASCADE AGAIN, but now EMPLOYING THREE CLOTHS 17

SOPHISTICATED MOVES and CASTS in the OVERALL CASCADE PATTERN 20

OTHER JUGGLING PATTERNS 24

BEAN-BAGS 30

VARIATIONS with BEAN-BAGS 34

JUGGLING with BALLS 37

FURTHER TRICKS with BALLS 39

BOUNCING BALLS on your HEAD 42

FEATS with PLATES 44

ROLLING a PLATE 46

WALTZING 48

SPINNING PLATES on POLES 50

ADVANCED PLATE TRICKS 54

A FENCE of SPINNING PLATES 56

HAT-TRICKS 62

FURTHER DOFFING and DONNING FLIPPANTRY 66

REARWARD DOFFING and DONNING 68

ROLLING your "TILE" 70

SOPHISTICATED HAT MANOEUVRES 74

BALANCING FEATS 78

MISCELLANEOUS FEATS of SKILL 86

INTRODUCTION:
AN ADMONITORY ANECDOTE

n my church in Slough, dedicated as it is to *St. Wilberforce*, whose name be praised, I was several years ago about the business of making the peace with my Lord when I came across a man of tattered apparel standing directly before the altar, drenched in the blue light from the GREAT WEST WINDOW (for it was afternoon), tossing high above his head an arc of differently-coloured baubles, moving so swiftly through the air that they seemed as a continuous stream of some bright liquid.

"My man," I said to him forthrightly; "What is it that you do in the House of the Lord?"

"Sire," said he: "I am but an humble layabout. I have no money, nor no worldly belongings, nor even a fixed abode, that I might offer our Great Lord in his Goodness. All that I have is mine artistry in juggling, and it is this which I would wish to offer to my God."

I was, as you may imagine, dear reader, at a loss for words.

I left him there, and called for a maid to summon the constabulary, and had him conveyed to the Marshalsea, where for all I know he still may be. There is a time and a place for everything, after all.

ARMYTAGE WARE, M.A. (OXON), D.D. (ST. ANDREWS)
THE RECTORY, SLOUGH, ALL HALLOWS' EVE, 1889

JUGGLING *with* SCARVES, NAPKINS *or* KERCHIEFS

ALMOST ALL of the juggling manoeuvres that can be achieved are adaptable in such a way that it makes little difference (within the bounds of commonsense!) what the objects are that are being juggled. However, some objects are easier to manipulate than others: rings and plates are quite thin and so, taking up little space, are less likely to collide with each other in the mid-air; whereas clubs and knives are regarded as exceptionally difficult "props" to use in juggling, as they must always be grasped in a single place, *viz:–* by their handle. Some of these objects move naturally through the air more swiftly than others; but this difference is in general so slight that it is barely to be noticed. Yet there are objects which move perceptibly more lethargically than their fellows; and this sluggishness is of great assistance in the learning of juggling feats and others requiring dexterity; for it enables the essentials of the art to be acquired before the extremes of pace must be encountered. And these objects are SCARVES, NAPKINS and UNSOILED KERCHIEFS. Thus we shall spend much of our time in this "manual" exploring the basic manoeuvres with kerchiefs; and let the other varieties of *"props"* – perhaps baubles acquired through confiscation from an indigent – be dealt with specifically where the means of manipulation differs.

Right from the utter start, it is the essence that you should comprehend that juggling is a matter of *rhythm*. In all that you do, establish a rhythm, and, once it has been established, adhere to it. Keep your God-given senses fully engaged in what you are doing; ignore any distractions from without; and concentrate on the pattern of the movements that you are making. They should be steady and systematic.

An early thing that must be learnt – and one that is not evident unless thought is brought to bear upon the matter – is that the objects you throw should be tossed *VERTICALLY*. This must become second nature to you. It is a frequent flaw in those who come anew to the art that they throw their objects not directly upwards but instead also a trifle forward, such that soon all is mayhem, as they must reach outwards to catch the descending "props" and thereby all rhythm is rapidly lost. It is therefore wise in the earliest stages of your progression to practise while facing a wall that is no more than your arm's length in front of you. Naturally you will have a disinclination (unless imbecilic) to smite this unyielding surface with your tender knuckles, and if you have not at first you will soon discover one; and so it will come to you that controlled and economical movements of your hands, enhanced by a verticality of upward toss, are a matter of instinct.

THE CASCADE

*T*his is the basic juggling move, and the one most often utilised in the juggling of odd numbers of objects. It incorporates throwing objects with a scooping underhand motion, such that they ascend across the front of your body.

Start (as you should start in almost all fresh aspects of the juggling art) with but a single kerchief or scarf, not a multiplicity as you will later manipu-

late. Take it by the centre of the cloth, and hold it in front of you, the back of your hand uppermost. Bring your arm across your chest, tossing the cloth such that it passes just above the level of your head; and catch it in your left hand, which is travelling downwards as it meets the cloth. Then, without any pause for the catching, continue the downward movement of that hand a

little, but bring it around in a small circle such that it is now travelling upwards as it reaches a position just in front of the centre of your chest; at which point the cloth should be let go, tossing it back towards the first hand. This hand should likewise have been making a circular movement, such that it is travelling downwards as it takes the flung cloth. Continue this *ad infinitum*, so that the kerchief follows an easy path, shaped like the numeral "8" laid upon its side; and do not allow your eyes to follow the kerchief as it traverses you repeatedly, but instead concentrate on knowing the cloth's trajectory through the regular and repeated, rhythmic swinging movements of your hands. This manoeuvre will soon seem to you facile in its banality and simplicity, yet persevere with it

a-while, for it is one with which you must become totally acquainted such that in future you may perform it without the chore of thinking (onerous to some of us at the best of times).

Once you have attained the blissful state wherein you perform this easily and suavely – yeah, and for long hours whilst also holding a conversation – the moment has arrived for you to progress one further small step up the long ladder towards the lofty heights of juggling mastery; for you are to take a *SECOND* kerchief, and establish a similar rhythm. Begin with a kerchief in each hand, and then get going. Each hand catches and releases the kerchiefs in the same positions as before; the sole difference is that there are now two kerchiefs, rather than but a single-ton executing the figure-of-

eight trajectory. You must throw, throw, catch, catch, throw, throw, &c.; with glibness and slickness. Watch the kerchiefs only when they are in the uppermost arcs of their trajectories; as before, it must become through the rhythm of your movements alone that you are ever aware of the position and motion of each of the twain cloths.

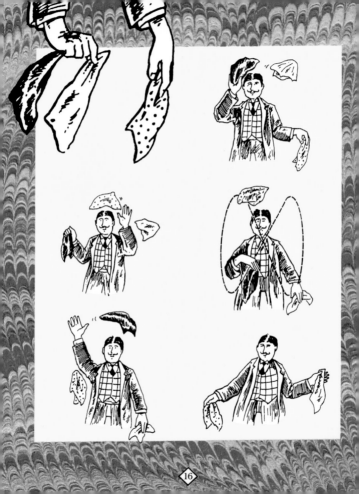

THE CASCADE AGAIN, *but now* EMPLOYING THREE CLOTHS

Now that you can throw TWO kerchiefs with the insouciance of an "old lag", it is time for you to encounter the CASCADE AS PERFORMED WITH THREE CLOTHS.

It will hardly need to be observed that the use of three objects of any sort in juggling necessitates there being a superfluity of objects over hands, there being but two hands given to each man.

To hold three kerchiefs with only the two hands, one hand must perforce hold two kerchiefs. This is done by holding a cloth, first, between the forefinger and the thumb; a second cloth may then be held between the remaining fingers and the fleshy base of the palm. We shall call these cloths One and Three, for reasons that shall unfold; cloth Two, the while, is to be held in your other hand.

Throw cloth ONE up and across your chest. As it reaches its height, cast cloth TWO, and keep the hand swinging around to catch cloth ONE, just as your first hand is swinging under to cast cloth THREE. Cloth TWO is at 🍂

this moment at the height of its arc, so the hand that has just thrown cloth THREE may easily swing around to catch it; the other hand is now moving to cast cloth ONE. Let not your gaze drop, but keep it always at the same height as that of the uppermost parts of the kerchiefs.

At first this is very hard to do, and you must not let your natural embarrassment and distress persuade you to abandon the exercise, for even the greatest of jongleurs started off in such a way. Besides, is not perseverance in seemingly unrewarded tasks a virtue? Your steadfastness will very rapidly be recompensed, for, as with one's first essays upon a penny-farthing, it is the initiation of the task that is hard; so that, once you have established your rhythm it becomes, like all other things in juggling, instinctual.

With some practice, you will be able to enter the CASCADE with three cloths smoothly and easily; and to continue it for as long as you will. The technique thus mastered, you may progress to its embellishment in sundry ways.

SOPHISTICATED MOVES *and* CASTS *in* *the* OVERALL CASCADE PATTERN

When you add an additional move to the basic pattern of the Cascade, beware that in so doing you do not disrupt the rhythm that you have established. Do not let your ambition rule your good sense, but progress cautiously; adding a new movement only as your level of ability enables you to do.

THROW UNDER A LEG

This is not altogether a manoeuvre fitting for execution in the presence of ladies and the youthful; yet it may raise many a merry laugh among men of the world, so long as the minds of all concerned are pure of intent.

In the course of maintaining the Cascade pattern, lift a knee so that the hand (with cloth) on that side may pass around the outside of the thigh and then up under it in a scooping motion, the cloth then being cast upwards, from this netherly position. You must make your cast quite forcefully, for the kerchief is starting lower and yet its path must attain the same height as normally; otherwise the catching hand will be forced to snatch at the cloth, and thus the rhythm of the pattern as a whole will be disrupted; and soon, of course, all will be a nonsense.

THROW BEHIND THE BACK

This is perhaps more difficult, in that the throwing arm must extend further, and the direction of throw is different, also. In one of its inwards and upwards circlings, bring the hand behind the body rather than in front of it. Once the hand is almost completely around the back to the other side, it may cast the cloth up *vertically,* not across, tho' perhaps a little forward also to compensate for the site of the hand at the moment of casting. The hand then swings back to resume its function in the Cascade pattern as a whole. It is hard to encompass this manoeuvre without breaking the rhythm of the arms' swing, and thus you will require a vast deal of practice before this move can with confidence be added to your repertoire. ❧

KICK-UP

Here you momentarily interrupt the steady flow quite deliberately, but then resume it precisely as before. What occurs is that you let a cloth drop until it almost encounters the floor, then interpose a foot (or knee) to instantaneously kick it back up vertically, so that at the weight of its trajectory, the cloth re-enters the steady Cascade pattern.

THE BARNUM & BAILEY
GREATEST SHOW ON EARTH

LaRoche

ERREMENTS DE LA SPHÈRE MYSTÉRIEUSE.
CETTE SPHÈRE MONTE ET DESCEND SUR UN PLAN
EN SPIRALE SANS AUCUN MOTEUR VISIBLE
TRIOMPHE AUDACIEUX ET NOUVEAU
REMPORTE DEVANT LES SPECTATEURS STUPÉFAITS.

L'INSTITUT DE DIVERTISSEMENT LE PLUS
GRAND ET LE PLUS MAGNIFIQUE DU MONDE.

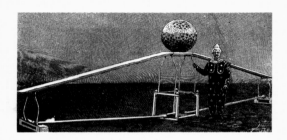

*O*THER *J*UGGLING *P*ATTERNS

THERE ARE. of course, a number of other juggling patterns, besides the Cascade, that may be adopted and, after practice, form part of your repertoire. Here are three which, while more suited to the juggling of solid objects – such as soft bags and baubles, which may be simply acquired from practising jugglers – can easily be done with cloths.

COLUMNS

This is, we adepts say, the simplest and easiest juggling move. Once you have it well practised you may progress to alternating between it and the Cascade, a translation that appears extremely impressive to your watchers; although it does require some concentration until you are fluent in the ability.

We shall assume that you are right-handed. Holding two cloths in your right hand, as indicated on page 25, and one in the left, cast first a single cloth directly upwards in front of your face. When this reaches its height, use both hands to throw up the other two kerchiefs simultaneously, one to either side of your head; as they in turn reach the top of their trajectories, your right hand should be in the central position, poised for the catching and re-casting of the first cloth. Then, as it in turn reaches its height, your two hands are catching the other two cloths and throwing them. Thus the three kerchiefs go vertically and down in three parallel columns, the singleton centrally, with the other two to either side.

THE SHOWER

This move is distinguished from those we have so far encountered, in that one hand – preferably the right – is responsible
always for throwing, the other hand having the sole function
of catching kerchiefs and passing them to the right. Thus each
cloth executes a circle, and once you have greased the translation of the kerchief from the left hand to the right by dint of
practice, the whole is maintained smoothly.

Start by using only a solitary cloth, and then progress to a
brace; thereafter the number that can be kept simultaneously
in circulation is limited only by your skill, although four is
regarded as admirable achievement.

SINGLE-HANDED JUGGLING

This art is much practised by veterans of the late skirmishings in the Crimea; but such is not to say as others may not enjoy it! Again the movement of the cloths is approximately circular; and again much practice is needful, especially in the fact that very rapid movements of the sole hand employed must be performed. Not only is the motion itself rapid; the hand must transmute in a twinkling from a catching to a throwing form. The latter action is somewhat tasking, although, for some strange reason, it has been observed that those of faulty vision take lesser trouble in adapting to the technique than do their wholer fellows.

TO JUGGLE WITH EVEN NUMBERS OF CLOTHS (THE FOUNTAIN)

Where four cloths (or six, or eight, for that matter, but let us not tax our credulities) are to be utilised, a new pattern must be adopted, and this is called the Fountain. In this manoeuvre, cloths are not caught and thrown by alternate hands, but instead fall always under the control of a single hand.

Start one's appreciation of this move by the use of only two cloths. The hands move in circles that are more-or-less parallel with your sides but a little outward to the front. As the hands come up in front of you (both at the same time) they cast the cloths up in the general direction of the centre – but not too much so, for the kerchief must continue in its general direction outwards. *At no time do the paths of the two cloths cross.*

Now try the manoeuvre with four kerchiefs, two per hand. Catch and throw the cloths alternately: as each pair reach the height of their arcs, the next pair must be launched; then, as the second pair approach their height, the first are being caught and cast; &c.; so that in fact you juggle two cloths with each hand, the cloths executing circular paths. This will appear to your audience to be a feat of intensely difficult execution; which is only just, because it is.

THE STAGGERED FOUNTAIN

The action of the Fountain is made to seem more fluid if, instead of being thrown in pairs, the casting of the cloths alternates from one hand to the next. Begin by throwing the first of the right hand's cloths, and then instantly cast the primary kerchief from the left. Then, throw the second from the right; then the second from the left. This staggerment of function is continued by the hands in the catching, as will seem natural, once the rudiments of the skill have been achieved.

BEAN·BAGS

A bean-bag is, as the name implies, a bag of strong cloth loosely filled with well-dried beans (usually haricot beans), peas or lentils. The material of which it is made must be sturdy – for a bean-bag will take punishment – yet it must also be soft and supple; and thus gabardine or worsted or some such-like cloth will be suitable, and serge ideal. The strongest of threads – an anglers' line may be utilized – is required for the sewing up. The bag may be cubical or spherical in form, the latter is, perhaps, better to adopt in the long run. The dimension of the bean-bag should be such as is most comfortable to the size of your hand, which will mean that for a cultivated person it will be in the vicinity of 3 inches across, and, for a manual worker or craven, 4 inches across. The bags are heavy enough and of sufficiently

flexible shape that they fall with a smack of pleasing firmness into your palms. They are easier to handle and to juggle than baubles, in that they do not tend to bounce out of your grasp; and thus they serve as a good introduction to the more difficult art.

However, bags are less easy to employ than kerchiefs, so you must return to the start of school again! Commence by practising with a solitary beanbag, no matter that it might look somewhat foolish. (A beanbag, stoutly hurled, impacts with satisfactory force . . .) A significant difference that you will at once find is that, whereas cloths are caught with the hand moving forwards and

downwards – like the pounce of a cat – the position of the hand in catching bean-bags is with the palm uppermost, such that the bean-bag naturally drops into it.

Now you are able to progress to the use of a brace of beanbags. As before, the two objects are cast upwards across the front of the chest, but their greatest altitude should not exceed one foot above your head; imagine that there is a breakable chandelier not far aloft, and you should find little hardship in this self-discipline. But the rhythmic pattern of movements is much as it was for the cloths; and soon you will be able to manipulate a trio at one time; and so forth.

VARIATIONS *with* BEAN-BAGS

Once you can juggle three bean-bags with such consummate ease that no concentration is required, prove to yourself that this is indeed the case by doing other activities at the same time. Walk about, perhaps from one room through an open door into the next. Or sing a hymn to yourself (ensuring that all the while you retain proper reverence). If your imagination is parched for any alternative, perhaps even discuss the affairs of the day with your loved one; it has to be done some time.

Learn to vary the height of the simple Cascade pattern. A higher throw gives you a longer interval between each catch and throw, yet you must also be prepared to move your hands a greater distance, because the accuracy of the throw decreases with its greater extent. Also remind yourself that the time advantage gained by a higher throw is not nearly so great as you might imagine; because of the mysteries of CREATION — *which*

remain mysteries to any sane man, despite the adherents of the heretic Newton — a cast of twice the height will permit you an increased interval before the bean-bag descends to your hand of only about one-half that of the original. You should also try rendering your pattern ever lower and tighter; as you do so, your hands will have to move ever swifter and more dexterously; but this is no bad thing — indeed, the exercise will be of value to you.

We saw that one of the qualities bean-bags have that goes unshared by baubles is that they do not bounce; indeed, they flex their form, if loosely filled enough, and will wrap around whatever it is they may land upon; and this can be used to inject variations into your pattern. For example, catch a bean-bag upon your foot or knee (as with a cloth), and then kick it upwards to rejoin its fellows. The like may also be executed with the head, although this is more exacting, as the head may not much upwards cast the projectile; yet it may be used to lob it forwards and thus back into the remainder of the pattern. PRACTICE MAKETH PERFECT.

JUGGLING *with* BALLS

The bouncelessness of a bean-bag was expressed as an advantage earlier, as indeed it is in the exercises best suited to bean-bags; yet a skilled juggler will regard the bouncefulness of baubles as likewise an advantage; for it may be used to add variations not possible with any other species of "props".

If you have mastered juggling with three or four bean-bags, the transition to utilising balls or baubles need not be difficult. Beware their bouncefulness; curl your fingers a trifle to dissuade the ball from flitting from your hand (but do not grasp firmly, as this hinders the movement). Use the *Cascade,* the *Columns,* the *Fountain,* the *Shower* and the *Staggered Fountain* techniques as described previously: each will seem a mite strange at first, with the new variety of projectiles, but soon you will become accustomed to them.

In addition, you might now desire to add the REVERSE CASCADE to your repertoire. When in the Cascade, you catch on the outside and then cast from somewhere close to the centre; in the

Reverse Cascade this is contrariwise, for you cast on the outside and catch in the middle, while maintaining a similar figure-of-eight pattern. Assist yourself by conjecturing that there is an open canister in front of your chest, into which you intend to cast your balls; but, in fact, there is, of course, no such canister; and thus you must catch the balls afore they drop.

❀FURTHER TRICKS *with* BALLS❀

BOUNCEFULNESS is not the only characteristic of balls; they also roll. Yet it is from the bouncing that you may extract the greatest means of astounding your watchers. You may use bouncing as a sort of upside-down juggling, in which the direction of your cast is downwards; the baubles spring upwards from the floor. Be sure to use balls, or baubles, that bounce well; croquet balls are not only unsuitable, but they also fracture the parquet.

FORCE BOUNCE: This is like the *Cascade*, but of course upside-down. Throw each ball down in front of the space between your feet, so that after the bounce the ball continues up to your other side. The pattern of casting and catching is exactly as for the Cascade; and so it should not take you long to learn, once you are acclimatised to the oppositeness of the direction of all your movements.

For especially impressive effect, place a drum in that area where the balls will bounce. Thus your audience will not only be dazzled by the speed of all the balls' motion; but will also delight in being deafened by the tattoo you cause to be beaten out.

FOLLOW THE LEADER: This may cast your mind back to the *Shower*, in that one hand is devoted entirely to casting, while the other is occupied in catching and then passing to the casting hand. Otherwise the similarity is not so great, for each ball will bounce twice betwixt cast and catch, something that would not be possible were the casting to be upwards.

Hold two balls in what will be your catching hand and a third in what will be your casting hand. Cast the third, or singleton, downwards and a trifle towards the centre; not too much, for the baubles will bounce twice, not once. Pass the

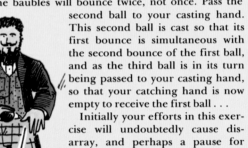

second ball to your casting hand. This second ball is cast so that its first bounce is simultaneous with the second bounce of the first ball, and as the third ball is in its turn being passed to your casting hand, so that your catching hand is now empty to receive the first ball . . .

Initially your efforts in this exercise will undoubtedly cause disarray, and perhaps a pause for entreaty from on High; but persist, for once the skill is gained it will take a little longer to attain easy proficiency.

BLONDIN THE WONDER OF THE WORLD

TRAINED AND PERFORMED BY COTTRELL

BOUNCING
BALLS *on*
your HEAD

With only a comparatively small period of practice, it becomes possible to bounce a ball or bauble in a continuous rhythm on your head. Use not the occiput, or top of the pate, but that part of your head where the hairline begins (*or did!*). By regular small, nodding movements, you will find you can, through practice, keep a ball bouncing there for several minutes at a stretch without causing you anguish. It is easier to gain accomplishment with a larger FOOT-BAUBLE, such as urchins use in soccer, and the effect can be all the more impressive to your spectators for the size; although conversely a very small, feather-light bauble, such as a PING-PONG BAUBLE, may likewise astound through its very frailty. Either way, soon you will become so adroit in bouncing baubles on your head that you will be able to continue doing so throughout performing other juggling acts with your hands; but ensure that there is a similarity of rhythm in both of these discrete sets of actions, as otherwise confusion may arise.

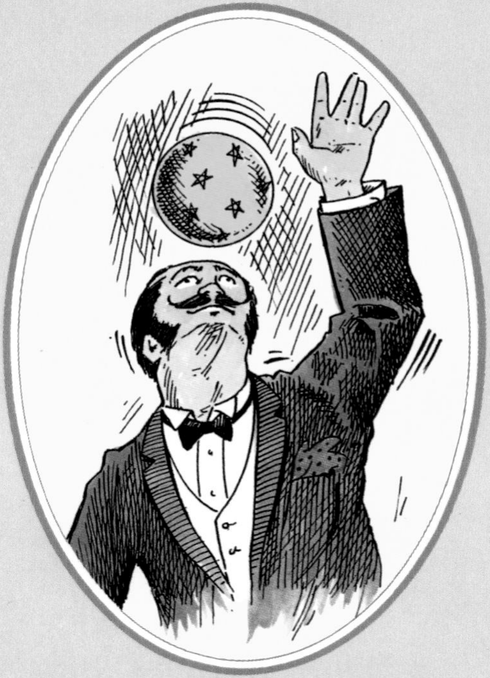

FEATS with PLATES

For the purpose of heightening your audience's delight and excitement, the tyro juggler may next advance to the manipulation of plates; and in so doing inspire in the audience the anticipation of the possibility of disaster, should one of these fall! Young eyes will shine with that combination of eagerness and dread! Yet, of course, your watchers will not know that the objects so tantalizingly pirouetting through the air, seemingly defying gravity, are not the SUNDAY WEDGWOOD, but rather the servants' dishes, and thus thin, light metal articles, painted in enamel and of little value.

To grip the edge of a plate, place it between the outer part of your forefinger and the inside of your thumb; your other three fingers, too, should be touching the rear of the plate, their function being to stabilise the grip.

Plates may be juggled rather as with balls; their thinness means that they are less likely to collide, and their shape is such that you may with confidence throw them higher. Once you have practised with a single plate until you are

knowledgeable of its behaviour, progress to the use of two. Spin each plate as you toss it aloft; then, as it reaches its highest point (or acme of flight), toss its fellow. Keep the palms of your hands inwards, facing each other; they will be at shoulder-height as you catch each descending plate. Once you can persuade two plates to dance their aerial fugue with aplomb, progress to three.

ROLLING *a* PLATE

Impress your audience by rolling a plate along one outstretched arm, across your chest, and then along the other arm, to your other hand. In truth this feat is not hard to perform, once you have practised a-while. Learn to flick your wrist *just so* as you release the plate, and the stability of your posture and the natural roll of the plate will do all the rest.

In similar wise, a plate may be tossed so that it lands on your upper arm, then roll itself obediently back along the arm to your hand. As you toss the plate, give it a spin, as if to make it bowl away from you; yet your throw is upwards, so that the plate, on landing, rolls in the intended direction. In a reverse way, you may easily learn to throw a plate to the floor some distance in front of you, so that it returns to your feet, like a fond dog.

WALTZING

For this performance, the dishes of your home's domesti-
cated animals, being of better and heavier quality, will be
better for your purposes than those used elsewhere. You must
also have a table that is quite perfectly flat and horizontal; if
there is a thin rim of some sort around its edge, then so much
the better (*your gardener may possess a Spirit-level, with which the
exactitude of the table's horizontality may be the more finely attuned*).
Your aim is to persuade an array of plates to dance – that is, to
spin vertically – together!

Spinning a plate in this way is not difficult, yet it is not done,
as you might conjecture, by use of the fingers together with
the thumb. Instead, the feat is executed by supporting the
plate vertically on the table by balancing it under a single
finger (usually the forefinger, yet the second may be pre-
ferred), and then twirling the finger in a circle; at which the

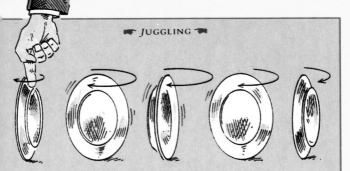

plate will start to do likewise. By increasing the rotational velocity of your finger, the plate will again increase its turning likewise; until the plate is vigorously a-spin, and will continue so after your finger is withdrawn.

Practise with a single plate until the art is learnt, returning your finger to the fray each time the plate begins to show the least sign of uncertainty in its rotation. Then attempt the feat with two plates kept *"WALTZING"* at once; and thereafter three; and so forth until you have, perhaps, mastered the achievement with a half-dozen or more. Both of your hands may be employed, though plates spun at first with the right hand are better continued with the right; and so with the left hand; as otherwise you may inadvertently try to spin a plate in the wrong direction.

SPINNING PLATES *on* POLES

*H*ere you will be glad of having first purloined metal plates from the servants' quarters; for the Dining Room *Spode* will not well withstand the indignities to which, in the early days, you must subject your equipment.

Your intention is, of course, that a plate should spin atop a blunt-pointed stick or cue; chopped short, billiards cues will serve ideally. As for the plates, these must now be amended by the gardener (or such other servant as will keep his peace about the dishes'

provenance for half-a-crown). With a hammer and some patience, and a plate set face-down, he must slowly beat the plate so that the bottom surface, once flat, becomes concave to form a smooth hollow – when the plate is turned right-ways-up, there will appear a conical convexity – or distinct peak, at the centre.

Your plate thus readied, you may toss it in the air with a flamboyant spin imparted by a flick of the wrist, and catch it on the end of your rod. The cane's point will settle in the

peak of the underside dip; and the plate will spin as if your balance and acuity were perfect.

This skill alone will be sufficient to amaze your spectators; yet, once your confidence has increased, you may choose to take matters one step further: to wit, spinning common or garden plates. For this you will require plates whose undersides are recessed, with a marked rim, as is not uncommon. Rest the plate on the tip of your pole in such a way so that the cane tip is against the inner side of the rim, and towards you. Then, with your free hand, give the plate a strong spin, yet not so strong that the tip of your cue leaps the rim; with the wrist of your other hand, make compensatory circular motions, such that the spin of the plate is reinforced.

In the early stages of your practice, many plates will fall. Have your free hand anticipatorily poised to catch such descending crockery, or, at worst, to fend it away from your face. Particularly you must guard your teeth.

The barrel jump.

ADVANCED PLATE TRICKS

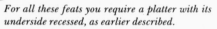

For all these feats you require a platter with its underside recessed, as earlier described.

Although it is barely more difficult in execution than catching a spinning plate on the tip of your cue, this technique fills many audiences with astonished delight. You cast a spinning plate off from one end of a stick and, as it soars, turn the stick so that the descending dish lands safely on the other end.

Clasp the pole at its centre, and practise first holding it thus with your plate a-spin on top. Then put aside your plate for the moment, and practise turning the stick. Rotate the stick downwards, so that its once-nether end now comes aloft, and adjust your clutch, pointing your forefinger down along the stick's shaft, so that you may still hold it easily vertical without

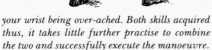

*your wrist being over-ached. Both skills acquired
thus, it takes little further practise to combine
the two and successfully execute the manoeuvre.*

   *Quite different, but far from hard once the
basic skills are yours, is the facility of causing a
plate to spin on the tip of your very fore- or
mid-finger, held vertically thrusting upwards.
As I say, this is far from hard, but the marvel-
lous effects are such as to amaze even stalwarts,
and small children may have to be led from the
room. The plate a-spin on its finger, you may
lift one bent leg and pass the platter aneath
your raised thigh; or, most profound of all, you
may pass the plate with one hand behind your
back, and there take it upon the raised finger of
your other hand, so that it re-emerges from behind you as if by miracle!*

A FENCE of SPINNING PLATES

          With some preparation – and much of the practice which brings men closer to godliness – you may create a marvellous palisade of upright rods, each bearing on its uppermost extremity a plate a-spin. For this you will require first the purchase of suitable dowelling rods, a fistful of the which can be bought from most timber merchants for a shilling, and which are of diameter perhaps one-quarter inch and length five feet, or a woman's height. (For such purchases I make the habit of begging my good lady to come with me, for purposes of measuring.) The rods obtained, find a level tract of lawn of size sufficient for your needs, and press into the ground the tips of your poles, evenly spaced one from the next, until they are securely anchored.

    Now you must gain the expertise to spin a plate on such a fixed pole. This is easier, perhaps, than you might imagine. Hold the plate so that its rim is against the pole's tip, as is standardly done, and while one hand clasps the rod about its centre, start the plate spinning with the other hand. Whenever the plate ☛

wearies, its spin may be reinvigorated by manipulation of the rod, as at the outset; but the plate will continue unattended for longer than you might think, for the flexibility of the rod under the weight of the plate encourages the spin.

Once you have attained this skill, it is an easy matter to keep two plates aloft; and then to learn to have more in place all at a single moment. You may challenge yourself to add one fresh plate to the total number of your achievement with each fresh day's practice, until it becomes hard to do so. As you progress, your skill may outgrow your lawn; but it is possible that your neighbours will have become so astounded by your prowess that they will not grieve to sacrifice their fences or ornamental hedges to permit you further space.

An exciting moment

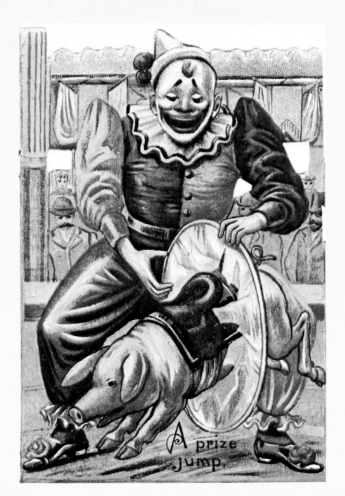

A prize jump.

HAT-TRICKS

Do you not recall the wonder with which, as an infant, you observed the skilled legerdemainist manipulate his proud Top Hat (or *Topper*, as the vulgar may describe it) during the performance of his other feats of Magick?

Such exploitations of the hat are not too exacting to initiate should the hat in question be of the correct variety; which is to say, it should be of sturdy construction and fairly heavy. A light hat is not so good. As your practice will be demanding upon the hat – for there will probably be much dropping – it is best to use one of little value to begin with, or perhaps one left on your rack by an acquaintance. Women's hats are unsuitable for all such exercises. ❧

⇜ JUGGLING ⇝

First, the DONNING and the DOFFING. No professional hatster would merely lift his "*tile*" in the conventional manner, except perhaps on entering the House of the Lord, but would instead do as I shall describe. In the doffing, place your right arm out in front of you, slightly to the side, with its palm facing upwards. With the other hand, reach casually behind your head, and with your fingers closed together, strongly flick the brim upwards. (Gloves will circumvent any pain that might be felt.) This will make the hat leap upwards and forwards in the motion of a cartwheel. For perfection in the rendition, practise so that the leading brim first lands upon your shoulder; then the leading edge of the crown bounces from the inside of your elbow; the trailing edge of the crown likewise upon your wrist; and thus at last the brim settles safely into your grasping fingers. At each instalment of this pro-

gress the motion of the hat is assisted as needs be by additional apposite flicks of your body.

For the donning, all is reversed; in early practice, a kerchief bound about your lower face will prevent possible hurt. Grasp the brim of the hat with your hand so that the fingers wrap around into the interior; then flip the hat back towards your head easily, so that the trailing edge of the crown first touches you just behind the wrist; a further movement of your arm assures that the leading edge strikes you around the elbow; and so to your head.

FURTHER DOFFING *and* DONNING: FLIPPANTRY

*F*lipping your hat to your head is not taxing, but first the simple art of flipping (by which we mean casting a hat so that it somersaults once or twice in the air before reaching its destination) should be learnt. This is easy enough from one hand to another. With the fingers of your right hand, clasp the brim of the upright hat on the right side of the brim. Then toss the hat by jerking upward with the hand, so that the brim, during the traverse, rotates about the crown; thus, as the hat reaches your left hand, the brim will have performed a complete vertical cartwheel. Such manoeuvres could be mas-

tered by even a child, yet they are exceedingly effective and may be employed to add a certain *frisson* of magick to your performance.

Now the similar may be executed, but this time with the top of your head, and not your left hand, as the target. Once this is mastered, learn to do so with such confidence that you need not duck your head nor watch the performance of the hat; in other words, until the trick is presented in such an everyday manner that it seems as if dexterity seeps from your very fingers. And finally, to pile wonder upon wonder, you may attempt the performance with the hat executing two rotations while it is airborne.

REARWARD DOFFING *and* DONNING

Here is an exercise that will test your skills of HAT MANIPULATION! *It gives a fittingly spectacular finale to all performances. First, toss the head backwards (the hands together behind the waist) in such a manner so that the hat, its crown touching once against the spine, rotates down to be caught by the hands at the rear. Then, as you bend forward in a bow to your adulatory spectators, flick the hat strongly back upwards, with the wrists and fingers, so that it reverses its previous progress, now travelling up the back, its crown striking the spine and the leading edge of its brim the rear of the neck, until it falls exquisitely upon your head — as neatly as if placed there by a* MONARCH'S MILLINER.

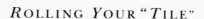
ROLLING YOUR "TILE"

hat may be rolled in a similar way as with a plate, albeit the exercise of balance is more intricate, the reason being that the hat, brim vertical, is not such a near-symmetric object as a plate.

A worthy trick to render is to roll a hat along one outstretched arm towards your head; then permit it to continue rolling so that it traverses your back about or

a little above the shoulder blades; and so down the rear of your other arm to your awaiting hand.

Hold the hat outstretched, its crown pointing behind you, and toss it a little in the air, giving it a profound flick with your wrist so that of its own accord, on landing, it rolls along your arm; raise your arm to an angle so that gravity may assist this rolling. Duck forward as

the hat nears your head, while also outstretching your
other arm so as to extend the downward-angled line of
its fellow. Your body should now be posed so that the
route from the fingers of your upraised
arm all the way down across your
shoulders to the fingers of your other
arm is but a single straight
line. Your lower arm you
will require to twist a little, so
that your hand is readied to
accept the rolling hat. All of
this is, in fact, less hard than
it might seem.

SOPHISTICATED HAT MANOEUVRES

ONCE THE ART has been acquired of flipping a hat so that it tumbles through the air to your head, there is no necessity that your head be always the target of your aim. You may, should you so wish, toss it on to the head of another; for instance you could make your audience marvel as the hat travels in a twinkling to surmount the occiput of one of their number. It is wise to practise this manoeuvre initially with a hatrack or other fittingly stationary object; and this target may, too, have advantages not negligible; in especial should you be one of those blades that works in an office, for such an embellishment to your doffing shall impress all, employers and employees alike. ✒

You may wish to don your hat by way of upwards flicking as afore, yet now, rather, instead of starting with the hat held out in front of you, you may wish to take it behind your back, and beneath your other arm, and then toss it headwards.

The catching of a hat need not be by a hand or a head or a hatrack: rather you may wish to impale it upon your knee or elbow or foot; from which such vantage it may, again with much by way of practise, be launched towards your head. Of these devices, the flip from the outstretched foot is the least difficult of execution.

Once kicking a hat from your foot to your head has become a matter of triviality for you, it is possible to add a further gaudy elaboration, one that is popular in the Americas. Rest the hat on your toes, but now, balance on its side a *large cigar*. Then flip the both of them upwards with your foot, and as the hat tumbles merrily towards your head, the cigar may cartwheel likewise to your awaiting lips. MUCH PRACTISE IS REQUIRED!

All of these skills may be combined with those that you have learnt through juggling kerchiefs, or baubles,

or plates. Thus, for example, you might be juggling three hats aloft conventionally as if they were but baubles, while interspersing this (with sophisticated synchronicity of timing) with casts of a further hat from your head to a foot and *vice versa*.

BALANCING FEATS

It is the fate of all innocuous pastimes to be, not merely the potential victims of the DARK ONE, but also to be the prey of science, and, far worse, of scientists.

As God has given it to all of us to know,

balance and poise are innate and instinctive attributes of those of requisite breeding; yet the scientists describe it in terms of *"FORCE VICARS"*, and *"VICAR TRANSFERS"*, and *"VICAR TRIANGLES"*, and the infernal like. Not the least loathsome expression in their pidgin is *"CENTRE OF INERTIA"*; which, should you incredulously ask them what it is that they are talking about, they will explain with the ill-placed condescension of a layman pretending to knowledge of mathematics, is the same as *"CENTRE OF GRAVITY"*. "Centre of hilarity, rather!" I always riposte to these sorry souls, which leaves them speechless. The location of the centre of inertia within an object, so they say, is what determines how easy it is to balance it, and how best it is to be balanced. Thus a long, thin and passing weighty object, with the bulk of its weight uppermost (and thus a high location for the centre of inertia), is easier to balance upright than a shorter, lighter one. It is as wise, therefore, ignoring such scapegrace *"explanations"* but accepting the evidence of one's senses, to learn the skill of balance through first employing some long object of this type.

Perhaps one of the billards cues (or similar) that might otherwise be in use for the spinning of plates.

The position for the first balancing is with the palm outstretched in front of you, the cue resting thereon. In order to maintain verticality, you will find that you must needs make some small compensatory movements for its tendencies to tilt; such movements should be from side to side, and not to and fro; indeed, in all feats of balancing objects on your limbs you shall find that side-to-side movements are better than to-and-fro ones, as these latter will swiftly become exaggerated, so that your object totters. (Through all of this, your body as a whole should be held as close to a perfectly motionless equilibrium as is possible; and your limbs should be steady.) In these adjustments, try to maintain the top of the object in stasis, as if 'twere hinged to the empty air; with only the lower end, and your hand on which it rests, being

mobile – and your gaze should therefore always be fixed upon the object's uppermost end.

Once the balance of the cue is child's-play to you, have the gardener saw six inches off its thicker end, and learn anew; such balance will be more difficult to accomplish with the shorter object (because, say the *"scientists"*, the site of its centre of inertia is proportionately lower), yet, owing to your skill already acquired, it will not take you long to triumph here. Once done, take a further six inches off the weightier end, and a further bout of prac-tice, until, in the course of time, you may balance an object no longer nor weightier than a pencil upon your outstretched palm.

Two ways are now open to your further progress. First, there is the route that leads to the balancing of objects whose con-figurations are vastly more complex than those of a pencil. Second, there is the

balancing of objects upon parts of your body other than your palms (your chin, or your forehead, or your nose), or even, through the precision of their placing, on a table or the floor – as in the instance of balancing a chair upon one single leg. Practice will make perfect; yet bear in mind always that, unless your aim is perfection for its own sake, you make a greater show through performing with an object that, though exotic, is in fact easy enough to balance, than through trying to poise something which, though humdrum, is yet very difficult. A long, broad, coloured feather – such as of an ostrich, or one plucked covertly from a peacock – is full easy to hold in balance, for God has willed that such things be reluctant to

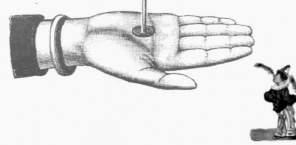

move other than slug-
gishly through the
air in any direction.

Very considerable
effects can be created
through balancing a
collection of objects.
Once you have learnt
to appreciate these
objects *as an aggregate*,
and once you have
made yourself aware
of the willingness
they have to slide
upon their shared
surfaces, then balan-
cing such assemblages
is scarcely more diffi-
cult than if they were
but a single object.

1642

Pet. Breug. inv. Hondius fecit.

C. privil.

MISCELLANEOUS FEATS *of* SKILL

THERE ARE many tricks, not all of them requiring much by way of skill for their execution, that you would be wise to add to your repertoire; for they may be used in the context of other and more onerous feats to make all about you seem in some wise magickal, as if you possess powers and abilities that are beyond the merely human.

THE CATCHING OF COINS
Bend back your arm and place upon it, near the elbow, a little pile of coins. In one easy movement, snap your open hand forward and downward so that you catch the coins as one. Little practice is required for this performance; yet the feat is a pleasingly impressive one.

Greater skill needs to be garnered for another coin-catching exercise. Here three coins are laid on the back of the hand in a line leading from the base of the fingers towards the wrist. When tossing the three in the air, it is possible to flick the hand in such a way that the coin furthest from the fingers flies

highest; and that nearest the fingers, least; thus the three coins, as they descend, may be caught by individual snatches of the hand at the air. Hard, dour practice will teach you this ability far better than any instruction could.

Should any of your audience question the expertise necessary for the execution of this feat, pray they try it for themselves, but with their own coins, for these latter will likely become lost in diverse corners of the room!

BALANCING AN INVERTED BOTTLE ON THE RIM OF A PLATE

This feat will appear to be well-nigh incomprehensibly difficult. Indeed, its mastery is not one that should be contemplated by the faint-hearted; and yet it need not be as hard as it seems. For, the wise virgins among jugglers will beforehand implant a rough-ended cork into the neck of the bottle, such that the roughened edge is just a whit proud of the glass; and thus the rim of the plate will be little likely to slip.

Bottle

REMOVING A TABLE-CLOTH WHILE YET ALL UPON IT REMAINS AT REST

This is not an after-dinner trick, no matter how tempting the moment might be; because it depends upon the use of a perfectly flattened, smooth table-cloth, without any creases or hidden impediments (such as congealing spots of gravy) that might disrupt the execution. The trick itself is no great shakes in terms of skill or dexterity; all that is required being the ability to remove the cloth in one fluid yet abrupt movement, so that the objects thereon remain in their position. Practise awhile in privacy and with items of less fragile mien, until you are sure enough in your abilities that you may conduct the exploit on a more elaborate scale.

THE ARCH-DEACON'S APPLE-AND-FORK TRICK

I include this feat, should any readers be sufficiently slack-

witted as to wish to perform it. Take an apple, and place it in the fingers of your right hand, the fingers being held lower than the rest of the hand. Now, on the back of the hand, balance a fork upright, the tip of its handle against your skin and the tines uppermost. In a single movement, cast your hand upwards, adding a flick with your wrist and fingers so that the apple soars and the fork flies less high. Catch the fork swiftly by its handle and thus be enabled to spear the apple adroitly as it descends.

BALANCING AN INVERTED VESUVIUS!
This is no trick for the tyro; nor should it be performed in a chamber that is too small. The day before you wish to astound those who would confound you, form from a sheet of newspaper a cone shape, folding it off so that it has a flat rim. Then, douse six inches or so of its sharper end in heavy brine (the more salt the better!) until it is well saturated; then put aside to dry. On the Great Day, light the wider, airier end of the cone with a match, and balance the cone with its sharp end on your chin, or forehead, or nose. The balancing will indeed be very easy (although your spectators will not realise that this is so), not only because the shape of the cone is such as to assist balance, but also because the burning newspaper will resist toppling, being drawn, as are all things burning, towards OUR MAKER. The burning will cease on encountering the salted portion of your cone; and you may take your bow.

The Annetty's

LES CROISIT

NOUVEAUTÉ SPORTIVE

DANS LEUR SCÈNE
AUX TEMPS DES CROISADES

FINIS

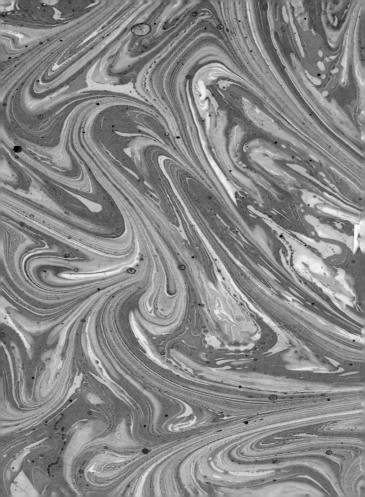